Incantations

of a wild heart

V. J. Markham

For my little wildling Tilly,

Xxx

To the readers who found my words,

Thank you for running wild with me.

X

To see a world in a grain of sand

And a heaven in a wildflower,

Hold infinity in the palm of your hand

And eternity in an hour.

-   WILLIAM BLAKE

Contents

Untamed Love

Love is the season that I fell for you, touched by the burnt Autumn of your heart, we were golden in our letting go.

Falling is a forever kind of feeling, knowing the landing will change the view, that the landscape will never hold the same earth,
but I could not reach you where you fell.

You will always be the slow burn that nature gives in the colours of its love, a season of fire and falling that my heart has gathered from its scattered place.

A love that taught me that even nature must change in order to let go and that I should learn how to catch myself first.

Perhaps he had not anticipated

the feelings he had stirred

when he touched upon her pages

a woman between words

You open my heart

and love pours out

where once there was

only blood

\-   *In the rush of feeling*

You dreamt of me
and I caught you
a w a k e n i n g
my heart

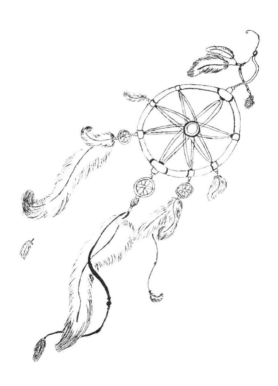

There are pages

inside my skin

holding my history

and you

become a part of the story

when you touch me

-    *Book*

I carry your name
within the skin of my words
that shed your letters
over-blankets of pages
cushioned for your landing
a bed where I can rest you
when I long to lay down
beside the weight of you

We belong here

in this moment

running wild

and

chasing dreams

Tied to love
a heart of ribbon
that rips wide open
to those it's given

I am as wild

as the sun

in full bloom

often too much

to be around

but filled with

a love

that does not know

when to stop

g i v i n g

And in a flash

we brought to light

the desire

we've been hiding

-   *Seduction of the storm*

I look for love

in the most

darkest places

like the moon,

hoping to be

held with more

then hands

with someone

that can finally

reach me

I am always afraid to admit

that I fell in love

with the night

in you

addicted to chasing after

your stars

You take my breath

and wear it

a heart wrapped in

the breeze of bones

from my chest

kissing it back to me

s l o w l y

giving life where once

it was taken

Your landscape

gave way to my earth

the only love

that has ever moved me

to my core

You have always had
a forest in your heart
the way you promise
so much adventure
and a shelter to return.

And in the thick of it
I am running wild

I was always drawn
to the wilderness
the places that make me feel
most alive.

You may only
know the silence
of your nature
but I hear you
when you are weary

Even tree's bend in the wind

You feel like a

b e g i n n i n g

I have never

touched

a lifeline hoping

to avoid the cracks

and maybe this time

we'll find a way

to keep on reaching

for the parts of us

that want to stay

Holding on does not always have to hurt

With each new layer you

discovered

I learnt to be truly

uncovered

You were the awakening
my bones craved
folded into corners
that suffocated
until I unravelled
to meet you

I creaked new life
into a fragile frame
mine or yours
(maybe both)
and together
we learnt how
to move past
the ache
of old spaces

Let me wander
into the wastelands
of your heart
I promise to plant
seeds in the cracks
and watch how
your world
begins to flower

Take my hand
and run with me
feel the Earth move with us
with each footstep we make
the ground becoming firmer
within our frolicking wake.

We were made to roam together
upon this feral land
sink your feet in deeper
and see how you still stand.

I have always wondered
how my words fold around
each other
to make poetry
the same way we did
limbs entwined
speaking in tongues
to create something
beautiful

There was magic

in the way he knew

how to read her

without saying a word

- *Connection*

Soft in nature

wild in love

I was a hive
to hold your love
in pools of golden honey
that tasted sweetest
upon your lips
when pouring thick
and runny

You released
these butterflies
within me
and in your kiss
they tickle
as they fly free

I think loving you

was never meant to be

s o f t or s m o o t h

but the kind

that creates a *shift*

between

being set on fire

or drowning

In all the ways
to touch you
the only way
that matters
is the way
my soul
collides
with yours

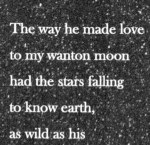

V.J. Markham

The way he made love

to my wanton moon

had the stars falling

to know earth,

as wild as his

I still love you

    even now

  when you cannot leave

      your shadows

        the stars know

          what it is

            to be in love

              with something

                only the dark

                  can hold

My words are not
my own
but rather planted
by your seed
and grown
into wildflowers
that roam
looking for space
to call home

Touch me in all the places

others were afraid to go

There will always be a

WATERFALL

within me

waiting to fall

for the one

who can cradle the

o u t p o u r i n g

I only love in waves

And I was always certain

that Autumn

was a time for

letting go

until I learnt

that it was in our nature

to bare all

for the things we love

I lay here blushed

from all the moments

you touched

my stem

in order to pick me

-     *Flower bed*

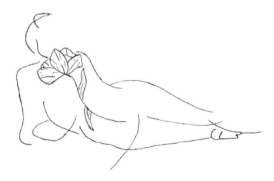

I have never been afraid
to dig my hands in deeper to you
and find dirt clinging
underneath my fingernails
like residue of old ghosts
soiling my hands
still, my fingertips
roam the roots of you
tracing the hidden parts
to find where it all began

Let me plant new life within you

We are fire and ash
made flammable in the heat
of wanton desires
laying claim to burning hearts
in our wild natured love

And like the body of flames
we scorch into one another
our embers scatter to the Earth
to rest spent in the soil sheets
we have made dirty

At once I knew for all I'd searched
that before you I had yearned
for everything that was not taught
that within you I had learned

I have longed to lay claim
to a part of your story
a place that only I exist
in the lines between
writing and written
can I be found.

And in my hope
I live in pages once blank
now holding your narrative
I have become the beginning
and the end of it all.

We are always wanting

to grow roots

in one another

but with you

I hope only to be soft

and hold you

for as long

as you need me

\-   *Moss*

My eyes

have always been

fireflies

dancing in the dusk

of your afterglow

Are we not all

c o n j u r i n g

magic

in the sound of our love?

-       *Incantations of a wild heart*

What came naturally

was the wildest love

of all

And I have seen us
in every colour of the sky
for nothing touches the Earth
quite like the atmosphere of love

She was chaos

and to love her

is to lose yourself a little

in the madness

But isn't that what love is?

a kind of wild

that settles in your heart

that no one but her

could tame.

Where the heart leads

the footsteps follow

- *Soul(es)*

I was the fruit

you picked too soon

crushed red on lips

in the heat of June

missed in an instant

by the hungry afternoon

You will always be the colour

of love

the only thing that suits me

Before you

I lost my words

with you

I made new ones

We are written

   in the stars

     and read by the moon

       the sky's forever love story

If I could ask time to allow us one more day,

I would spend it in your arms forgetting tomorrow

existed between us.

For that is the thing with time and love,

they both keep giving, never knowing which one

will let go first.

I do not know

how to be timid

or *gentle*

with my love

I am the volcano

that erupted

when my heart

became too warm

I am explosive when I melt

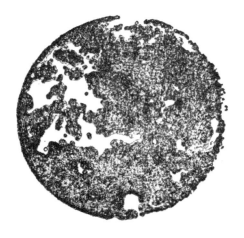

Leaving was never my intention

but all wild things must be set free

\-   *A conversation with the Moon*

She is the

landscape

that changed

your view

He leaves an earthquake

under my skin

the shudder of everything kissed

moving me on the inside

You hold me with your eyes

but love me with your mouth

- *In the face of us*

It was love in the only way you knew how

sometimes hidden

and

sometimes whole

Although time took from us

love still gave so much

You walk with me from time to time, hand holding like we never let go. Your callouses give away your struggles and my softness confesses my own.

The touch of you has always been seasoned with nostalgia, moments I can find us when I long to be held. I hope we always meet like this, on memory lane, maybe then you will understand how much I miss you.

For a fleeting moment, I remember the warmth
of your eyes, honey hues encased in bronze that
melted in one glance

The look of love they call it

And you wore it just for me

You called to the wild in me

and set me free

We collided like stars kissing earth
balls of fire that turned to sparks on impact.
the light of lust and love consumed us but did not
teach us how to burn out in a world afraid of
fire and ice.

Time may have left us counting stars from
the ground up but one day we'll fall again.

And when we do, we'll *fly*

They say that we are

twin flames

burning

for the other

and I know

I have never

felt heat

like the fire

you set ablaze

in me

-     *FATE*

The sun cannot exist without the moon and I
fell in love with your juxtaposed heart, for the
sky and I would be empty without both.

I have always been a madly

wild thing

and to love me is to let

the adventure begin

I hope the storm in my heart

made chaos in your own

for I left pieces of myself

that will move you

to all the places you need to go

You equate me

-     *The sum of our parts*

And even in your darkest shade

when the light seems

furthest from your skyline

I reach forward to remind you

of our sunset

and how even saying goodbye

still holds the warmest glow

She had the world

in her eyes

the most beautiful wild

he'd ever seen

We have become a tidal wave

rushing into one another

and calling it love

when really we only meant

to wash up and meet the shore

and leave our wounds out at sea

And now the salt of you

is what is *healing me*

.

Like magnets

we remain attracted

fighting against the pull

a parallel force

destined to seek

longing to hold

Whatever our substance was made of

we were always destined for chemistry

Maybe this just is

and we just are

and for now

maybe that is enough

For once it is written

ink becomes blood

an imprint of time

the mark of our love

I draw a line

from you to me

knowing the distance

will only separate us

if we cannot

meet in the middle

-    *Expression of the equator*

They said the world was flat until they discovered it was
round, as circular as life, a never-ending beginning.
With you, I understand the meaning of discovery and
how like the Earth, we never really stop spinning when
love is the journey.

Long story short

we were poetry

I try hopelessly

to grow away

from you

only to have

flowers

bloom in all the places

you touch

-    *In vain*

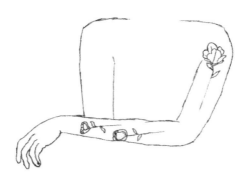

V.J. Markham

And on the nights

I long for you

the moon tells me

She misses us too

V.J. Markham

And sometimes our

s t a r s

are a reminder

of all we did

to light up

a dark world

to give the moon

H O P E

that she is not alone

Are we not

all running wild

behind closed eyes?

I have storms

within my skin

always chasing

the light

that comes

with the rain

gold is my favourite colour when you find me

\-   *RAINBOWS END*

This is not where it all began
nor is it all yet written.
Life is as wild as words
we learn to grow from both

- *Excerpt*

Wilderness

There is earth that does not yet know the touch of human hands, like the places within me that have yet to discover where the wild lives.

I sometimes cannot see the wood for the tree's when the light only reflects my shadows that follow my footsteps into the unknown.
There is so much pain in wandering, searching for a new way home to myself, in ways the Earth crumbles when more of its nature is taken away.

Who was I before the darkness seeped in and who will I be afterwards?

Becoming lost is the only way to be found, as wildflowers that push through the grit to surface from the shadows, so I must learn to grow from all that buries me.

Our atmosphere is changing

my Earth no longer quakes

from the touch of you

My yesterday

sang of you

the melody

of my broken tomorrow

Bittersweet the song

of melancholy

a sound so often heard

in voices calling

for the one

who never

hears a word

Once you were my favourite book, taking me to places I've never been, folding me into corners on those I have. I learnt new words to take with me to where I needed to be, lines that ran away from us onto pages new.

And so much like books, we had to return what we were given, our loving hearts on borrowed time.

Perhaps it was

moving forward

that she did not

want to face

I cannot go back even if I wanted to

\-   TIME

I let you go

in *p i e c e s*

the same way

you fed me

L O V E

for these

b r e a d c r u m b s

are your undoing

and the trail

H O M E

to *myself*

Watch

how **I**

e s c a p e

you

and tell me

it's not

magic

\-   *Sleight of hand*

You made yourself

a ghost

when you ignored me

so how can you

be indignant

when I no longer

see you?

I let you go

but I could not

hold on

to myself

we were the

S T O R M

that took it all

when it left

V.J. Markham

Haunted by
the crescent
I am half,
seeped in
convalescent
rising
from the dark

A wandering star

she moves through

darkened skies

bringing the moon

to its knees

in hope of holding her

from fate

but she belongs

to the night

bound to exist

only to fall

in a suicide of light

Our fingertips kiss

sometimes in hello

too often in goodbye

Feel my earth

the grit

that digs into my soul

soil that sometimes

is not watered in growth

but to drown my roots

from becoming

all I was meant to be

then tell me

if you could bury yourself

beside me

and love the darkest parts

the sunlight

never seems to reach

I will always kiss you

where it hurts

even if I swallow thorns

from roses

that came before me

I am not afraid

of a little pain

if it means

you'll pick me

My flower heart

grown from rain

that watered petals

red from pain

will you ever bloom

as pretty again?

You were like the seasons

forever changing

I always did

have an Autumn heart

falling for those

that let me go

Loving you

felt like rainbows

after a violet storm

that stripped the sky

from its grey

a promise

of better weather

But rainbows cannot

exist without rain

and my tears

can no longer

be the catalyst

for your light

WATCH ME

e m e r g e

from your

dirt

beautiful

in my escape

from your

darkness

We are never alone

in our heartbreak

the sky weeps

when the sun leaves

I think there will

always be

a part of me

that does not know

how to *give myself*

to another

without pain

\-   *Poison Ivy*

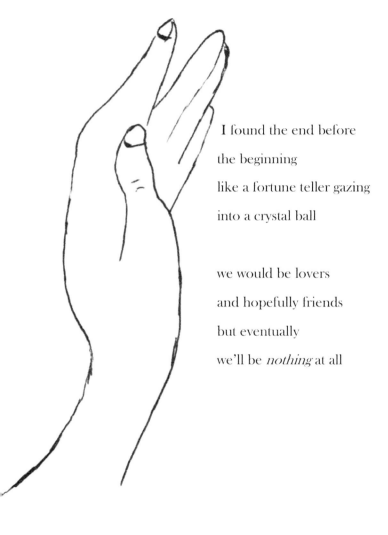

 I found the end before

the beginning

like a fortune teller gazing

into a crystal ball

we would be lovers

and hopefully friends

but eventually

we'll be *nothing* at all

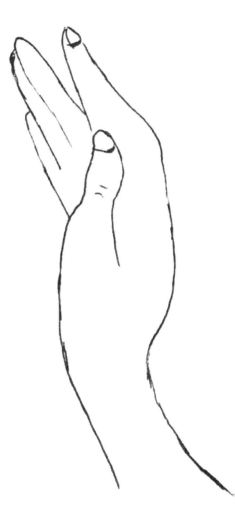

They call me a witch

for creating

M A G I C

with my fingers

but writing is a curse

I placed upon myself

to give beauty

to my pain

There was so much

darkness in you

that I could not see

the light

I slip slowly

from blood to ink

drowned in pages

wet from tears

that leave ripples

in my words

a puddle

of my own making

I cry with you

and I don't pretend

to know

your pain

just that you

need to let it go

and I can show you

the way

\-   RAIN

We no longer speak

the same love language

but I will never forget

the sound

Even the tree's

cannot carry

o l d w o u n d s

-    *Dead Wood*

They do not tell you what it feels like

to smile over cracks,

the corners of your mouth

crumbling

in the force of lips stretched

over sorrow.

And they commend you

for your strength

in the face of such struggle

wondering how you do it.

I wish I could tell them

what my truth will not,

that my teeth bite

to hold on

with every grinning moment,

a false pearl beauty

rotting on the inside

In the noise of the everyday

there is a silence

that speaks the loudest.

In a world

of 7 billion people

how is it I

feel so alone?

.

Let him be your last breath

and let him go

What I would give

for a heart

that is free

to beat

from its cage

Letting go

the art of

forcing

bones to break

a skeleton, once whole

now loves in fractures

My house

    will never be a home

        for him

           and yet

        even in his

        leaving

          I always

             make room

                for him

                    when he chooses

                  to stay

These walls
cannot stand
another goodbye
cracked and aching
from the settlement
of your leaving
my house called you
it's home

and so did I

I wanted you

to meet me

halfway

but sometimes

even that

is too far

Some days I feel

I am not enough

for myself

yet most days

I am too much

for you

I hold fire

in burnt hands

still learning

how to warm

myself first

Open me up

and you will see

I am made of Daisies

the kind that looks pretty

when he loves me

but always garlanded

in chains

when not

- *Euffeuiller la Marguerite*

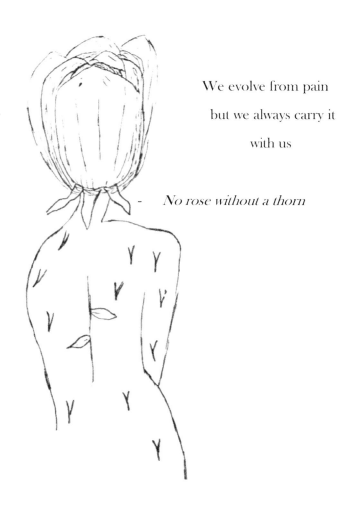

We evolve from pain

but we always carry it

with us

\-   *No rose without a thorn*

They asked me why

they could taste heartbreak

on my lips

and so I told them

that was the last thing

I kissed

with meaning

I wore regret

like my favourite lipstick

smudged onto hollow mouths

pink and puckered

for the sin of my sorrow.

Trembling lips still hold

the heaviest heartbreak

but mostly, they don't know

the difference.

They only want the woman

kissing the lie.

In the face of it

you will only see

the wounds of battle

painted on by war

-       *Make up*

Your soul

is my oblivion

lost to your

blackhole

I float uneven

out of control

and wild

for the love

that I believe in

And in his leaving

she learnt

he was never meant

to stay

I kept you always
at arm's length
and was disappointed
when you couldn't
reach me

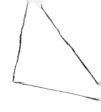

We envelope

into one another

folded at the corners

from hands not made

to read us.

Somehow, we are all

love letters

lost in translation

searching for those

who understand *how*

we are written

Vacant is the one who loves without the touch of
tenderness, a soul kept in glass eyes reflecting shadows.
Do you see the pain in the breaking of hearts left scattered,
like the love notes you scribbled on the back of receipts,
of an ordinary life you could not afford.

Vacant is the one who expresses love without the trace of
tone, a mouth that opens wide to swallow every part of
your flesh and bone, sticking your heart between canines
to chew on later if you become too wild for his taste.
Did you savour each kiss of life you gave to those you cut
open with your tongue, a bloodlust that only moved on
once the marrow had been licked clean.

Vacant is the one who never leaves his burial ground,
haunted by his ghosts of the past, to dig up old flames he
cremated and reminding them of the heat of his lust, for
everything twisted and burnt out.

Do you feel the emptiness from those who have found
peace in their afterlife, no longer living in a dying
breath for a love like yours to resurrect.

I wonder how it feels to be so vacant you no longer have
any power to be *seen* or *heard.*

Does her pain

glisten like diamonds

tears shaped like

shards of glass

every drop cutting

from the loss

of another goodbye

come to pass

and you wish you

could be the one

to end it all

at last

You may wonder

how you can hear

the crack

of your heart

after another

heartbreak

only to realise

that love

is never silent

It was a *s l o w* death

learning to let go

of what could not

survive

-    *The end of us*

In our garden
full of roses
you never let me
see your thorns.

How the colour rose
tints even the smallest
scratch

She was all thicket

and thorns

a wild woman

surviving the wilderness

learning to grow roses

from her pain

There are lights

you will no longer

see me in

fragile fragments of

a morning glow

upon my ethereal English rose skin

the fire of my mood

melting against hot embers of emotion

burning for your love

the bright beautiful smile

in my honey hazel eyes

that look upon your shades

with hope

maybe your viewpoint

cannot hold my shine

I see you in a new light too

Do not serve me a half measure

and expect me to feel full

We were

skin on skin

and still

it was not enough

to touch you

I break my own neck

hanging onto the hope

of your words

only to be strangled

by all the things

you don't say

I survived the w i l d

    in the same way

        you did

           so do not tell me

           you don't have

           c l a w s

           as sharp

           as *mine*

I wonder

if I had been more

would I have slipped

through your fingers

any less?

I placed my hands on your heart, the coal black veins
that fed its dark, as I tried to bring magic to its
chambers, to spark light in corners that hung webs
of shadow, where nothing had been living.

My alchemist fingers could not turn rhythm into
rhyme, nor bring the light into your ebony eclipse.
Sometimes gold cannot be made from human
heartbreak, sometimes love cannot penetrate *stone*.

I may be clouded

by my love for you

but I am always moving on

-    *Confessions of the sky*

One day

the closest you

will ever get to me

is the pages

of my book

and I won't feel

the touch of you

as you leaf through me

hoping to find

what you once left

I finally grew a spine.

Maybe I am the star

that did not fall

for his earth

there is love

in the letting go

of those too far

to grasp

V.J. Markham

We all must die

in the forest

to live

in the wild

I rose in light

to cover your

darkness

but you still

found a way

to survive

while I burned away

thinking it was love

-    *Sorrow of the sun*

Writing is the wound

that words weep from

and you

handed me the pen

Do not attempt

to train

the dragon in me

I breathe fire

because I have

been burnt

It was our time to shine

but neither could hold the other

with the same measure

in the same light

One day you'll pick up

the puzzle of your pieces

and another

will be the glue

that holds them all together

for I was always

just quicksand

that you didn't know how

to get out of

Perhaps the galaxy

within me

is why you needed

space

- *The truth in our stars*

And I broke

    like a storm

        for even the sky

            has its cracks

sometimes our clouds

        are too *heavy*

I lick my wounds

tongue twisted strokes

tasting wild

superficial scratches

bleed out your ego

my bare skin

just another trophy

you tried to claim

your instinct may always be

to hunt those you love

but your claws

can never hold down

the animal in me

The poison in your lips

killed us both

with a kiss

There was always an ocean of love

caught between tides

but so much like the sea

you rushed in

only to leave again

in waves

Even the sky

must find its place

in between the fog

and the fury

Those who lack depth

are destined to be shallow

Sometimes we get

caught up

in the illusion

of those

not meant

to love us

-    WEB OF LIES

We think

we pick our battles

wisely

So why

are we always

at war

with ourselves?

We view love with kaleidoscope eyes,

once so full of colour, often loses focus upon

reflection

A sheet of pale skin

fragile and gathered

cut white from the bones of my marrow

learning to fly in formation

as an aeroplane

or look as dainty as a swan

I am a bleached chameleon

now you see me

F L O A T I N G

F A L L I N G

F O L D E D

now you don't

a new me once again

the ever-evolving paper chase

Maybe it was

always going

to end

just another

season

we had to say

goodbye to

hopeful that

it would come back

for what it left behind

V.J. Markham

And maybe

we turn

c o l d

to save

what is left

from a

broken heart

-     *Winter*

We are all

a little broken

a little sharp

but you have to

smooth your edges

how can they

get close to you

when you always

make them bleed?

The world is under the weather

teaching the sky how to heal

We were hoping

   to find footprints

      of all the ways

         we used to move

            - *Treading water*

Ashen

we breed ghosts

from our pain

haunted

until we learn

where to bury it

Maybe you only

see me

when you need

something

to believe in

\- *Ghosts of the heart*

We are used

to holding

fragility

in our hands

and letting it go

as softly as it lands

without a whisper

of how it touched us

or how beautiful it was

before it left

When did we hide our wild

behind the wool society pulls

in front of our eyes?

\-   *A wolf in sheep's clothing*

Do not call us animals

because we have learnt

how to shed the skin

you branded weak

to become

the wolves of the wild

those that shift

Evolve

in ways only the moon

can understand

And despite

the goodbye in us

there will always

be a season

that comes back

for me

Autumn will always fall for me

in a way you never could

The Nature of me

Born from seeds suckling soil
I was dirty from the moment
I was made.
Buried before I knew how to grow
they passed me over like earth barren
gritty and wild
stubborn in the roots
how could she ever learn how to bloom?
A pretty petal
too scattered to ever be whole.

If only they knew I learnt how to let go
long before they could touch me.

She did not ask

for the wild

to save her

but it taught her

how to believe

in the nature

of herself

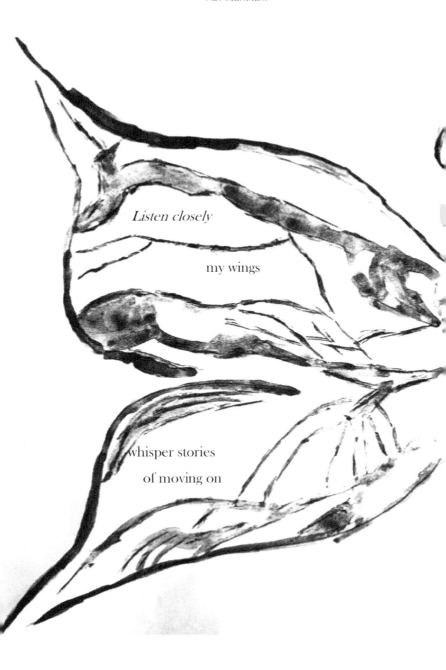

Listen closely

my wings

whisper stories

of moving on

I have my head

in the clouds

dreaming of all the ways

I could touch the sky

wondering how far

my wings

will take me

I make homes in inhabitable places

as if I could turn wild into welcome

and welcome into *stay.*

But I cannot grow everywhere

I try to bury roots

there is only so much shelter

from the storm

and even nature knows

it has to move on

from old spaces.

V.J. Markham

I cannot rise

in the darkness

wearing the day

of before

when I am forever

someone new

embracing the shape

of my phases

Chase the Moon

she is always

only a breath away

Let go of your rusted shades

falling only brings you closer

to where you *need to be*

There is simply

never enough light

to filter out

my darkest parts

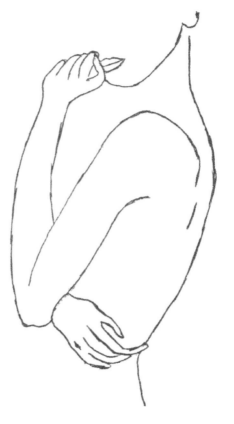

my s i l h o u e t t e

still holds

all my secrets

You were brave

because you

let it in

even when you knew

it could break you

love is fragile in the wrong hands

In this moment
I am more butterfly
then wolf
both transformed
into something
beyond moonlight
both clawing a way out
from our old skin.

And like the butterfly
I have learnt fragile
is a new strength
but like the wolf
I sill cry
when the world
turns dark

I am gentle

with my broken pieces

the ones that cut

when they fell

I have bled enough times

trying to fit them back together

I know now

to handle myself

with care

Once in a blue moon

I let my sadness show too

Maybe I am looking

to plant

R O O T S

in all the places

you think

I'll never grow

And on the days

I feel most alone

the moon stays awake

to remind me

that we don't all

have to live

in the dark

And when she gazes

upon you

with so much

light

you can barely

be so bold

as to look her

in the face

   -   SUN

Come back

to yourself

slowly

even the earth

moves in seasons

My scars are

constellations

a map of my

unfolding

the light of my

HEALING

I own my chaos

as mother nature intended

in the storm of my heart

free to rage within love

consumed in the rush of feeling

devastating pieces of myself

in the wreckage of wanting and needing

and in the aftermath

learning how to be a *survivor*

of my own debris

There is magic within these bones

a skeleton conjured from feathers flown

once soared in downy plumes to nest

a hopeful heart inside the softest chest

let love find its way home

Perhaps I am longing

for a wilderness

that understands

the nature of me

Someday those scars

will turn into butterflies

a beautiful reminder

of how far you've come

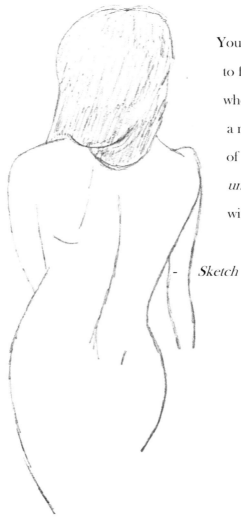

You cannot hope

to find my edges

when they are only

a rough outline

of what is still

unfinished

within me

\-   *Sketch*

Above water

they teach us

how to survive

but when drowning

we learn most

about being alive

Even the earth

    has us b e l i e v i n g

        in magic

      -   *Trick of the light*

I am always

finding

new ways

to grow

if you'll let me

- *Wild Woman*

As thunder longs

for lightening's kiss

be the storm

the clouds will miss

And like the sky

that opened up

it's tears

so I learnt how

to be seen

in the rain

As the light

is always searching

for a way to be found

so the dark

is always

wanting a place

to belong

V.J. Markham

You wear

your vulnerabilities

brightly

on the dark sleeve

of your canvas

knowing stars

will always paint you

in the best light

My mind

seldom knew

the way home

but my body

always found it

I am made

to understand

my ripples

my human

holds *reflection*

in my DNA

- *Body of water*

Weave your spirit

around bones in ruin

and feel the life

return, when moving

There was never a happy ever after only a story

and in the end it's the stories we remember

You have always been music

an ebb and flow of rhythm

echoing within the walls of you

a beating only you can own

that vibrates throughout your journey,

a melody humming to your song

that gives sound to the places you touch

a voice to those you resonate among.

How beautiful that you have the courage

to be heard when the world

is so often silent.

There is no greater thing

then the caterpillar who

grew wings

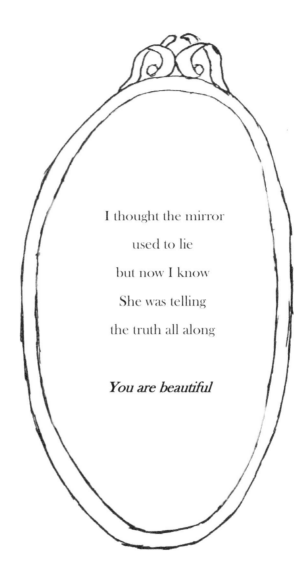

I thought the mirror

used to lie

but now I know

She was telling

the truth all along

You are beautiful

We are all just April showers, waiting to grow seeds

from our rain.

Maybe I was too much

chaos

in a world that only

understood quiet

There will never be things

left unsaid

with me

like the wild,

I find ways

to keep telling my story

even when more of me

is taken away

Too many times

they have trampled

on the vines

of my heart

and still I grow

through the ache

of my scattered petals

calling my bloom

home

I have a wildflower heart

finding light

in all the dark places

Maybe there is a reason

our heads are in the clouds

because we have to

reach up high

to meet our dreams

and know that nothing

is too big for us to hold

if the sun can touch

the edges of the world

so we can too

We learn how to

kiss fragility

with enough softness

it dances

when it is

set free

\-   *Dandelion*

Wild

is the woman

who comes back

to herself

no matter

how far

she wanders

Maybe letting go

is arriving somewhere new

a place that breaking

is only ever really

becoming

becoming more of you

There is no smoke

without fire

and I am known

to cause a flame

Like the cocoon

that I became

there was something

beautiful inside

all along

-       *Metamorphosis*

I promise to return

more courageous

than before

for the bravest thing

you can do

is learn to rise again

L I G H T E R

than the dark

they put you in

\-   *Spring*

The fire within me

still burns

even if all I can feel

is smoke

No matter how beautiful the flower
it is the stem that carries the weight
of admiration.

Sometimes we may bend
but we are always reaching

Like the moon
   I too am learning
      to love my craters
         left from impact

V.J. Markham

This Earth

feels so uneven

and I am still

learning

how to fall

with grace

V.J. Markham

The universe in you

will one day

find a place

that does not feel

too big

to be held

or too small

to be seen

235

Could you love a heart

made of glass

so fragile

that when warm

only knows

how to shatter?

If the sky

is the limit

then why am I always

reaching for the stars?

I am soft lighting

and springtime

fireflies mistaken

for falling stars

the staining of love

on lipstick smears

bookends holding on

to heavy edges

but mostly

I am dark ink

folded into white pages

finding a way home

I am not afraid

to chase you

if you promise

to catch me

-    *Hurricane*

Free spirit

wild heart

V.J. Markham

Call me a Rose

for I am every part

B L O O M I N G

and only

t h o r n y

when handled

without care

241

Remember your roots

they will still be *buried deep*

when they have finished

picking the petals from you

You long to swim

in the current of me

but I reflect depths

you were not ready to see

Maybe it is

a l c h e m y

the way we

transform

from broken

to beautiful

or maybe you

were G O L D

all along

Only you know the journey of your wings, the places
they have taken you and how they have always
brought you home again.
There is a beauty in the way you learn how to fly,
without ever knowing where you will land next.

Perhaps my light

has always been

a reflection

of my darkness

a glinting caught

between oceans

a ripple

of my depths

Tears only blossom

what is yet to grow

Made of thunder

she moved as a storm

a beautiful chaos

in her lightening form

They think a woman

who is made of soil

Only grows in dark places

but if they knew

how deep

she had searched

for herself

they would understand

why she is always so

dirty

The season may not

always be bright

but I have learnt

how to keep

G R O W I N G

in the storm

- *Evergreen*

One day

I'll step back to the

broken places

I've been

knowing how far

I've come

and making peace

with the ghosts

that live there

There is something

b e a u t i f u l

about the way

you keep searching

until you are found

-    *Hide and Seek*

V.J. Markham

Fearful

is the word

they give to the wild

Fearless

is the word

the wild

gives you

253

You were born

in the dark

maybe that is how

you learnt

to feel your way

through it all

\-   HEART

V.J. Markham

'Do not be so full of yourself'

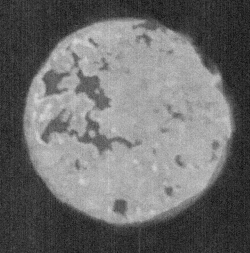

even the moon must face battles with the dark

Are we not all

S E A R C H I N G

for a place

to bury

ourselves?

\-   *Bookworm*

The thread of you

will only unravel

if you pick yourself apart

They don't want the girl
made of soil
they want the woman
in full bloom

do not let them forget
how you got there
let them see the root
of your pain
and the growth it took you
to flower

Where the wild lives

my nature survives

I fall in love

with storms

the kind that know

how to break

the silence

without fear

of being heard

V.J. Markham

Let love find you

in the dark

and remind you

that even stars

need shadows

to survive

She takes the form
of every wave
learning to move oceans
from her pain

I loved me first

so you could love me last

Maybe my beauty

is defined

in all the ways

my shades

reach you

for art

is made

to be given

away

She knew how to leave

without making a sound

the soil made a story

from her footsteps

\-   *Global footprint*

For she was home

in the wild of her skin

a woman in form

but a shapeshifter within

We are

always

b r a v e

when we fall

some things

are not meant

to last forever

-     *Stars*

You are

every reason

to keep going

so

r o o t e d

in hope

and

BEAUTIFUL

when you

let it

blossom

\-   *Wildflower*

To find the human in me

take a chance on my wild,

for we are one and the same

- *Nature and I*

About the Author

Verity Markham is a writer and mother from the United Kingdom. She has been writing since the age of 8, creating stories and bringing her imagination to life.

As an adult, Verity has found expression with her writing on such platforms as *Thought Catalog* and *She Rose Revolution* to bring light and healing to others from her own experiences, also being published in *The Cambridge Hall Poetry journal 2021, From the Heart 2021,* an annual collection of the year's most heartfelt poetry and awarded elite writer status and featured in *The Poet's Yearbook 2021.* Her first poetry collection **Incantations of a wild heart**, is inspired by her journey in love and loss, healing and the importance of belonging to herself first and foremost.

Find Verity on Facebook and Instagram **@v.j.markham** for more of her writing.